# THE
# TAMAR AND TAVY
# VALLEYS

## · A PAST and PRESENT COMPANION ·

London and South Western Ry.
———
787
WATERLOO TO
**LATCHLEY HALT**

London and South Western Ry.
———
787
WATERLOO TO
**CALSTOCK**

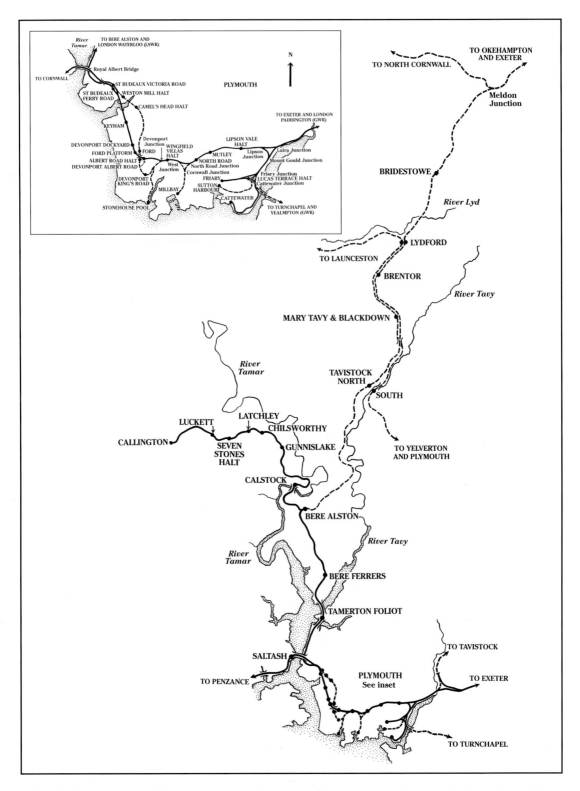

**Map of the Tamar and Tavy Valleys, showing the Plymouth to Okehampton and Exeter main line as far as Meldon Junction, and the branch line from Bere Alston to Callington.**

# THE
# TAMAR AND TAVY VALLEYS

· A PAST and PRESENT COMPANION ·

*A nostalgic trip along the former Southern Railway lines in the Tamar and Tavy Valleys*

**Terry Gough**

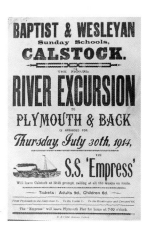

· RAILWAY HERITAGE ·
*from*
The NOSTALGIA Collection

First published in 2001

British Library Cataloguing in Publication Data

A catalogue record for this book is available from the British Library.

ISBN 1 85895 171 2

Past & Present Publishing Ltd
The Trundle
Ringstead Road
Great Addington
Kettering
Northants NN14 4BW

Tel/Fax: 01536 330588
email: sales@nostalgiacollection.com
Website: www.nostalgiacollection.com

Maps drawn by Christina Siviter

All items of ephemera are from the author's collection.

Printed and bound in Great Britain

A Past & Present book
from
*The NOSTALGIA Collection*

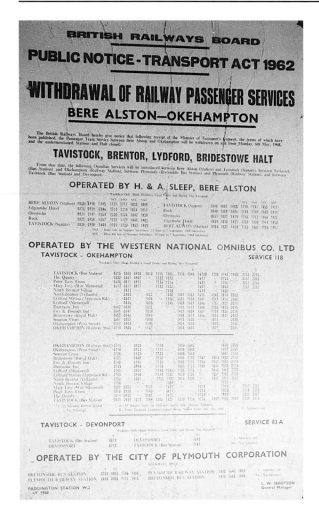

*Title page* **Before the opening of railway services between Calstock and Plymouth, people often travelled by boat. Excursions later offered a pleasant alternative to the train, and even today round trips can be made, one way by boat and the other by train.** *Calstock Parish Archive*

*Left* **Notices advising of the withdrawal of passenger services were all too common in the 1960s. This notice refers to the intermediate stations on the main line between Bere Alston and Okehampton and resulted in the severing of the main line between these two points. Replacement bus services ran between Bere Alston and Tavistock, and between Tavistock and Okehampton, but most did not connect at Tavistock and did not start from the same location in the town. The Okehampton bus took about an hour compared with an all-stations train, which took just over half that time.** *D. J. Aston*

# CONTENTS

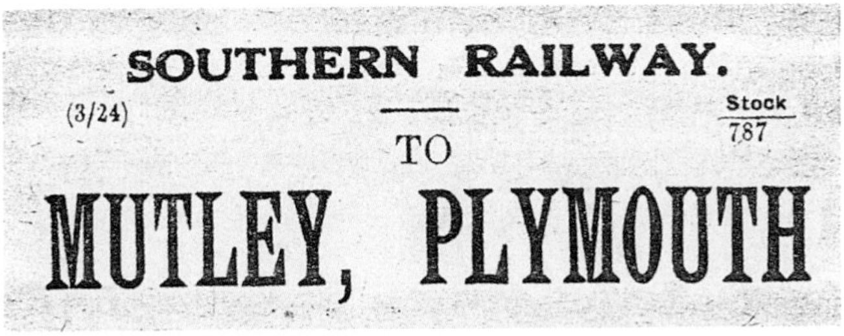

SOUTHERN RAILWAY.

(3/24)

Stock
787

TO

MUTLEY, PLYMOUTH

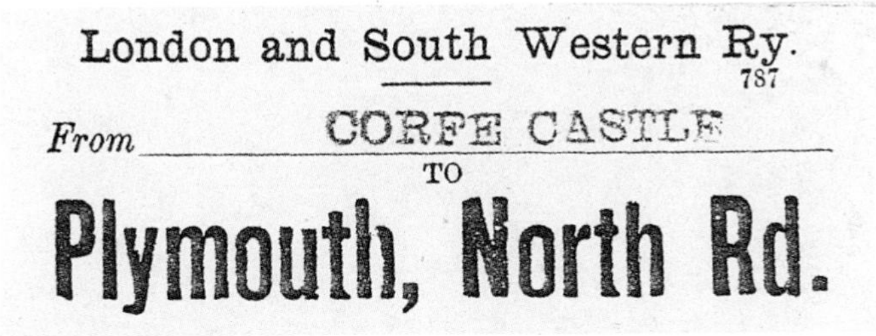

London and South Western Ry.

787

From _____ CORFE CASTLE _____

TO

Plymouth, North Rd.

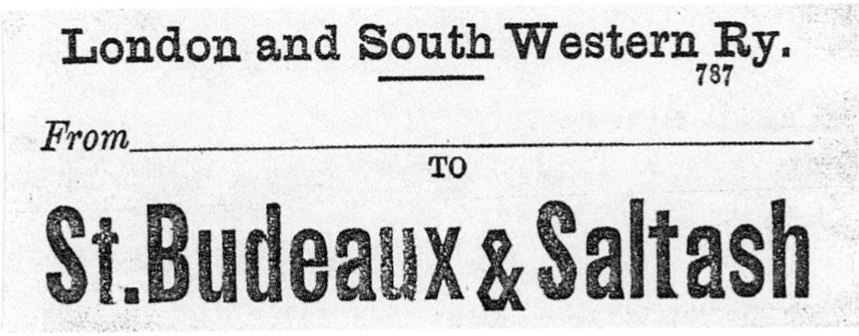

London and South Western Ry.

787

From _____

TO

St. Budeaux & Saltash

A Plymouth Friary to Tavistock train arrives at Bere Alston on 27 June 1956, hauled by ex-LSWR Class O2 No 30225. The coaches form Set No 15; next to the engine is ex-LSWR Brake 3rd No 2616 and at the rear is ex-LSWR Brake Composite No 6506. The trains for Callington left from the other face of the island platform on the right.

The scene today was captured on 5 May 1999 when DMU Class 150 No 150267 arrived on the 11.30 from Plymouth. All trains now use the old down main line, as the up main line and the branch bay have been removed. *J. H. Aston/TG*

# INTRODUCTION

For much of its length the River Tamar represents the boundary between Devon and Cornwall; its source is only 3 miles from the Atlantic coast, thereby almost cutting Cornwall adrift. The river flows through isolated parts of the two counties, past woods, agricultural land, villages and towns, deserted mines and other industrial sites, and ultimately to Saltash.

In the mid-19th century there were at least 17 mines within a few miles of Calstock, but over a relatively short period of time all but two closed. One of the largest was the Devon Great Consols on the east bank just above Gunnislake. These mines were connected in 1859 by a tramway to Morwellham (5 miles away), where the company had its own quay. Morwellham was close to Calstock geographically, but 6 miles by road. At its peak it was claimed to handle more copper than anywhere else in the British Empire. Calstock had its own quays for handling minerals from the mines, and was also a shipbuilding centre, with yards on both banks of the river, which were made redundant with the coming of the railway. Calstock thus suffered the double blow of the closure of the mines and the shipbuilding industry within a single generation. Market gardens were later established, particularly on the hills facing south toward the Tamar, and the produce was transported by rail. Almost all of these have since closed as a result of competition from elsewhere. There were several other quays further downstream on both banks of the river, from where minerals and other commodities were shipped down the Tamar.

The Tamar is tidal from New Bridge, which carries the main road from Tavistock to Gunnislake and Callington. There was no other road bridge across the Tamar below here until the Tamar Bridge at Saltash, carrying the A38 trunk road into Cornwall, was opened in 1962.

The River Tavy rises on Dartmoor east of Lydford. Lydford is famous for its gorge and waterfall on the River Lyd, which flows not into the nearby Tavy, but into the Tamar 9 miles to the west. The Tavy passes near the villages of Mary Tavy and Peter Tavy before reaching the market town of Tavistock. At one time this was a Stannary Town by virtue of the extensive tin mining in the area; there was also a thriving woollen industry and iron works. About a mile to the south of Tavistock is Crowndale, close to the river, where Sir Francis Drake was born.

A little further downstream, near Shillamill, a canal, opened in 1817, ran to Morwellham, thus connecting the Tavy and Tamar. The canal carried ore and many other commodities from Tavistock to Morwellham, with coal and other necessities being transported in the opposite direction. From the end of the canal was an inclined-plane tramway descending at 1 in 6 to the quayside. The coming of the railways and the decline in mining both dramatically affected business, and the canal ceased operations in about 1880. From Shillamill the Tavy runs through mostly wooded country until opening out just before Bere Ferrers. From there it is only 2 miles to Warleigh Point, where the Tavy flows into the Tamar. The only bridge over the Tavy between Tavistock and the confluence of the two rivers is at Denham, where a minor road links Bere Alston with towns and villages on the east bank. The river is tidal as far as Lopwell, about halfway downstream from Denham Bridge.

The potential of these two valleys for the construction of railways was realised in the mid-19th century. A line, which became part of the Great Western Railway (GWR), was built from Plymouth for the first few miles along the Plym Valley, after which it followed the River Meavy to Yelverton. It then took a north-westerly route through Tavistock as far as Lydford, where it turned west to Launceston. It opened from Plymouth to Tavistock in 1859 and to Lydford and Launceston in 1865. A line from Plymouth crossing the River Tamar on Brunel's Royal Albert Bridge to Saltash was also opened in 1859, and this became the GWR's main line into Cornwall. Trains ran from a terminus at Millbay until a joint GWR/London & South Western Railway (LSWR) station was opened at Plymouth North Road in 1877.

The LSWR line from Okehampton to Lydford opened in 1874, crossing the West Okement River at Meldon and running along the north-west edge of Dartmoor. From 1876 the LSWR ran trains to Plymouth using the GWR line from Lydford via Tavistock (later named Tavistock South) and Yelverton, and approaching its own new terminus at Devonport from the east. The Plymouth, Devonport & South Western Junction Railway (PDSWJR) was formed to build a line from Lydford to Plymouth via a new station at Tavistock (later named Tavistock North), and this opened in 1890. It followed the GWR line close to the River Burn, then the River Tavy from about 2 miles north of Tavistock, and continued to follow the Tavy past Crowndale as far as Higher Gawton (4 miles from Tavistock), where it turned south-west toward Bere Alston, an isolated town trapped between the two rivers; at this point the railway was equidistant from the Tavy and Tamar. It continued to Bere Ferrers, also between the two rivers, then 1½ miles further on it crossed the Tavy at its confluence with the Tamar. It then ran along the Devon bank of the Tamar before reaching the LSWR station at Devonport. Devonport thus became a through station, with LSWR trains arriving from the west by means of the new line (which was leased to the LSWR) and terminating at the joint GWR/LSWR station at Plymouth North Road. The LSWR had a goods depot at Plymouth Friary and this was opened to passengers in 1891 to become the new terminus for the company's trains.

A narrow gauge line, the East Cornwall Mineral Railway (ECMR), was opened between Calstock Quay and Kelly Bray (near Callington) in May 1872, although it had been operational for several years prior to this. At Calstock minerals were loaded into barges for the journey along the Tamar and thence to South Wales or overseas. The company was taken over by the PDSWJR in 1891. In 1908 the PDSWJR opened a branch from Bere Alston to Kelly Bray, using much of the former ECMR line, which it converted to standard gauge. The branch did not form part of the LSWR, but retained its separate identity until it was absorbed by the Southern Railway in 1923.

The LSWR lines also became part of the Southern Railway in 1923, and the Southern Region of British Railways in 1948. In 1950 all former SR lines were transferred to the Western Region, then back to the Southern Region in 1958, to return to the Western Region in 1963. At the time of writing the remaining services are operated by Wales & West, but this is likely to change in the near future with the creation of a Cornwall & Plymouth Business Unit.

Contrasts abound in the Tamar and Tavy Valleys. I have endeavoured to show this in the photographs, taken at the beginning, middle and end of the 20th century. Wherever possible I have taken the present-day photographs from exactly the same position as the archive ones, thus emphasising the changes that have taken place. I have included photographs of the railways, the towns and villages in the valleys, the mines, and the rivers themselves. Changes over the years have been extreme, as the mining industry declined, the railways were built, the rivers ceased to carry commercial traffic, and tourism increased. But one aspect of this area has not changed, seen at one time as a drawback, but now increasingly as an advantage: its isolation caused by the lack of good road access. There is no possibility of this changing because of the geography of the valleys, so the area has been spared the havoc brought by the motor vehicle to so many other beautiful parts of the country. Despite wholesale closures in other parts of Devon and Cornwall, it has also meant the survival of part of the railway system, precisely because the most direct access to the area is by rail.

I have concentrated on the railway lines of the former Southern Railway that ran in both the Tamar and Tavy Valleys, but this book is not exclusively for the railway enthusiast. It is for all who have an interest in the Valleys, which in 1995 were designated an Area of Outstanding Natural Beauty. The photographic journey starts in Plymouth, because this is where most present-day visitors will begin, at least if travelling by train, and I have included the former GWR main line in the Plymouth area only where this is used by the present-day train service in the Tamar Valley. It is no longer possible to travel by train to Tavistock and Okehampton, although there seems a likelihood that within the next decade train services as far as Tavistock could be re-instated for use by commuters and visitors.

All that remains open today is the section from Plymouth to Gunnislake, which gives beautiful views of and ready access to the Tamar Valley. Although a day trip to the end of the line is well worth while, it is also good to alight at the intermediate stations and explore the villages and surrounding countryside on foot. There are combined rail and river trips between Plymouth and Calstock during the summer months. It is also well worth visiting Morwellham Quay, where there is much of interest. There are several walking guides and these are listed in the Bibliography. There are also books on the history of the valleys, in particular on mining and shipping, as well as local museums, and archive collections for more serious study.

On Mondays to Fridays there are eight trains each way on the Tamar Valley Line, seven on Saturdays and five on Sundays (during the summer only). On summer Sundays a co-ordinated bus and train service is run across much of the territory once served by the SR. This is an excellent way of visiting the area, with Okehampton being used as the connecting point between the train from Exeter and the various bus routes, one of which takes passengers to Gunnislake to meet Tamar Valley trains. Some of these buses go via Morwellham Quay. There is also a train service between Okehampton and Meldon, from where a little of the old LSWR line can be walked over Meldon Viaduct toward Bridestowe. On weekdays there are four buses per hour from Plymouth to Tavistock, with on average one per hour continuing to Brentor and Lydford (and beyond), thus giving access to the Tavy Valley.

**Terry Gough**
**Sherborne, Dorset**

**Note**
Over the years the spellings of some place names have changed and I have taken the later versions used by the railway companies. Examples are Lidford and Lydford, Beer Ferris and Bere Ferrers, Cox's Park and Coxpark. 'Wheal' is a Cornish term for 'mine', while the term 'consol' refers to a consolidation of companies. Railways usually close on specific dates, advertised in advance. On the other hand, the closure of mines was much less precise and many continued for years at ever-reducing output before being abandoned. As a result there are some variations in closure dates between the different sources of information I have used.

# ACKNOWLEDGEMENTS

I am grateful to the various photographers whose names are credited in the captions. I also thank Tony Bates (King Street Curios, Tavistock), Patrick Coleman (Calstock Parish Archive), Ann Eade (Callington Museum), Gary Emerson (Morwellham & Tamar Valley Trust), Yvonne King, Doris Sleeman and the late John Smith (Lens of Sutton) for the provision of information and archive material. I also thank the various landowners who kindly granted permission to enter their property to take photographs. I appreciate the help given by my daughter Anna of Plymouth and, as always, my wife Cynthia.

# BIBLIOGRAPHY

**Transport**
Bastin, Colin Henry *The Plymouth, Gunnislake and Callington Railway* (C. H. Bastin Publishing, 1990)
    *By Train to Okehampton* (C. H. Bastin Publishing, 1995)
Cheesman, A. J. *The Plymouth, Devonport & South Western Junction Railway* (Oakwood Press, 1967)
Crumblehome, Roger; Gibson, Bryan; Stuckey, Douglas; and Whetmath, Charles *Callington Railway* (Forge Books, 1997) ISBN 0 904662 23 3
Fryer, Stephen *The Building of the Plymouth, Devonport & South Western Junction Railway* (Stephen Fryer, 1997) ISBN 0 9529922 0 5
Gough, Terry *The Kent & East Sussex Railway, A Past & Present Companion* (Past & Present, 1998) ISBN1 85895 149 6
    *The Tarka and Dartmoor Lines* (Past & Present Publishing, 1998) ISBN 85895 139 9
Hawkins, Mac *LSWR West Country Lines Then and Now* (David & Charles, 1993) ISBN 0 7153 0122 5
Mitchell, David *British Railways Past & Present No 8: Devon* (Past & Present, 1991) ISBN 1 85895 009 0
    *British Railways Past & Present No 17: Cornwall* (Past & Present, 1993) ISBN 1 85895 001 5
Parkhouse, Neil 'Building Calstock Viaduct' in *Archive*, Issue No 2 (Lightmoor Press, 1999) ISSN 1352 7991
Roche, T. W. E. *The Withered Arm* (Forge Books, 1977)
Semmens, Peter *Railway World Special: The Southern West of Exeter* (Ian Allan, 1988) ISBN 0 7110 1806 5
Thomas, David St John *A Regional History of the Railways of Great Britain, Volume 1: The West Country* (David & Charles, 1981) ISBN 0 7153 8210 1
Trevelyan, Robert E. *A Winter Remembered, No 2* (Ark Publications, 1998) ISBN 1 873029 08 X

**Town and country**
Barber, Chips *Along the Tavy* (Obelisk Publications, 1998) ISBN 1 899073 68 X
Beddow, A. J. C. *A History of Bere Ferrers* (1975)
Booker, Frank *Industrial Archaeology of the Tamar Valley* (1974)
    *Morwellham Quay* (Jarrold Publishing, 1994)
Bryant, Betty and Clamp, Arthur L. *Portrait of Tamerton Foliot Village, Part Two* (1983)
Callington Local History Group *Callington Town Trails* (1988)
Coleman, Patrick E. *A Guide to Calstock* (Ecosouthwest, 1998) ISBN 0 947748 00 8
Eade, Anne *Kit Hill Our Hill* (Columbian Press, 1989) ISBN 1 871330 02 5
    *Kit Hill Aureole* (Columbian Press, 1993) ISBN 1 871330 06 8
    *The Town under the Hill* (Columbian Press, 1997) ISBN 1 871330 23 8
    *The Mines of Calstock and Callington* (Callington Museum)
Foot, Sarah *Following the Tamar* (Bossiney Books, 1980) ISBN 0 906456 35 5
Furneaux, Rob *Rambles around the Tamar Valley* (Ex Libris Press, 1994) ISBN 0 948578 59
Herring, Peter *Archaeology of Kit Hill* (Cornwall County Council, 1990) ISBN 1 898166 82 X
King, Yvonne Pellow *My Village – Luckett* (1993)
McCallum, Denis *Walks in Tamar and Tavy Country* (Obelisk Publications, 1992) ISBN 0 946651 63 9
Paige, R. T. *The Tamar Valley and its People* (Dartington Amenity Research Trust, 1984) ISBN 0 905926 06 4
    *The Tamar Valley at Work* (Dartington Amenity Research Trust)
Patrick, Amber *Morwellham Quay, a History* (Morwellham Quay Museum, 1990) ISBN 0 9516360 0 6
*Tamar Valley Discovery Trail* (Devon County Council, West Devon Borough Council and Tamar Valley Countryside Service)
Trounson, J. *Mining in Cornwall, Volume 2* (Moorland Publishing) ISBN 0 903485 95 8

**Ordnance Survey Maps**
First Edition (1865) Tavistock and Plymouth (reprinted as sheets 90 and 97 by David & Charles, 1970)
Fifth Edition (1931), Sheets 137 and 144
New Popular Edition (1946), Sheets 175, 186 and 187
Landranger Series (current), Sheets 191 and 201
Explorer Series (current), Sheet 108
Outdoor Leisure (current), Sheet 28

# Departure from Plymouth

A view looking toward the buffer stops of Plymouth Friary station, probably taken in the 1930s. Passenger facilities were modest, but there was an extensive network of sidings for carriage storage and goods traffic. The station closed to passengers on 15 September 1958, although the station building remained intact until 1976. All this has since been swept away and the only landmark is the church spire in the background. *Courtesy Lens of Sutton/TG*

*Right* A platform ticket issued after transfer of the station to the Western Region.

Looking east, away from the terminus, Plymouth Friary engine shed can just be discerned in the distance, to the right of the main line. Today much of the Friary site is leased for industrial use, although some of the track is still in place and was used by stone trains during 1999. The loop is still used by diesel shunters that work bitumen trains to Cattewater. *Courtesy Lens of Sutton/TG*

This was the view from the side of the engine shed looking west toward the terminus on 11 July 1924. The train is the 12.15pm to St Budeaux and is hauled by Class O2 No 230. The coaches are an LSWR 'gate' set, so named because the centre exits were protected by iron gates rather than doors. These coaches survived into British Railways days and examples could also be seen on the Yeovil Junction-Town-Pen Mill local trains. The line on the left was the branch to Turnchapel, and a few yards behind the camera was Lucas Terrace Halt, which was served only by the branch trains.

The engine shed has been demolished but the halt still exists, although it closed on 10 September 1951 when passenger services were withdrawn from the branch. The branch beyond Cattewater Junction closed entirely 10 years later. The freight-only line serving Cattewater was also accessed from the branch. On my visit in May 1999, there was clear evidence of recent use of both the branch and main line in the vicinity of the halt. These lines formed two sides of a triangle, with the old main line and a third line leading to Laira, where the GWR had its own engine sheds. The site is now occupied by a diesel and train maintenance depot. *H. C. Casserley/TG*

Friary engine shed replaced an earlier building in 1908. It was transferred to the Western Region in 1958 and was closed in May 1963. In BR days it had an allocation of approximately 25 engines, from the Class B4 0-4-0 dock tanks to Bulleid 'Pacifics' for express trains. There were also two identical 0-6-2 tank engines from the former Plymouth, Devonport & South Western Junction Railway, which were used mostly on the Callington branch trains until 1952. One of these engines, No 30758 *Lord St Levan*, is undergoing repairs outside the shed on 15 April 1956. Both were transferred to Eastleigh later in the year, and after a little use were scrapped. A third PDSWJR tank engine, an 0-6-0, had left the area in 1931 for London, where it was used on shunting duties until withdrawal in 1951. All three engines carried the names of people associated with the Company. The same location in 1999 shows the outside wall of a fertiliser storage depot that has replaced the railway buildings. *Both TG*

After briefly running alongside the River Plym, the LSWR main line swung sharp west past Laira to join the GWR main line from Exeter toward the centre of Plymouth. There was a halt at Lipson Vale (closed on 22 March 1942) and a station at Mutley (closed on 3 July 1939), which was built by the GWR and served by both GWR and SR trains. On 8 July 1924 an LSWR train in the hands of a Class T9 4-4-0 passes through Mutley en route to Friary.

Remnants of the station still exist and many of the houses seen in the 'past' photograph still stand. The large building in the right background is an eye infirmary, which opened in 1901 and is still in use. A multi-storey car park of particularly ugly design has been built over the railway and mars what is an otherwise pleasant area. This photograph of Class 47 No 47737 *Resurgent* on an up Royal Mail train was taken from the car park on 7 May 1999. *H. C. Casserley/TG*

At Plymouth North Road trains for Exeter and London departed in opposite directions, no doubt to the confusion of passengers. From 1891 all LSWR and later SR trains from Friary calling here left in a westerly direction, while GWR and later Western Region up trains headed east out of North Road. A Friary to Exeter train, hauled by 'Battle of Britain' Class No 34069 *Hawkinge*, enters North Road in the early 1950s.

In the spring of 1999 an infrastructure train double-headed by Class 37 Nos 37521 and 37153 enters the station. The site of Mutley station is just round the corner where the terraced houses are on rising ground. *Mike Esau/TG*

On 30 August 1945 Class M7 No 24 leaves North Road on the 4.05pm from Friary to Tavistock, using the LSWR route via Bere Alston. Present-day services to Bere Alston (and on to Gunnislake) still start from North Road station, which has been rebuilt and the track layout simplified. The suffix 'North Road' was dropped following closure of Friary.

The two views are matched with the aid of the platform access lift housings. On 7 May 1999 Class 150 No 150267 forms the 13.47 to Gunnislake. On the right is Class 153 No 153312. These two platforms are bays, and are end-on with similar bays facing the opposite direction that are used mainly for Royal Mail traffic. *H. C. Casserley/TG*

# The LSWR route to St Budeaux

The GWR and LSWR had separate lines from Devonport Junction, just west of North Road, to St Budeaux, where they had their own stations. There was also duplication of stations serving intermediate locations. On the LSWR line the first station was Devonport King's Road, a large structure that was the original LSWR terminus for trains from Exeter and Okehampton. Just before the station was a goods yard, and on 30 August 1945 Class O2 No 216 is on shunting duties. This was also the junction for the Stonehouse Pool branch, opened in 1904 for LSWR boat trains from Waterloo; this service was withdrawn in 1911, but the line continued to be used for goods traffic until 1966, closing completely in May 1970. On the extreme left is the main line, the beginning of the branch being the line immediately to the left of the engine. This area is now a car park and the only reminder of the railway is the iron footbridge that spanned the yard. *H. C. Casserley/TG*

**G.W.R.**

**Devonport S.R.**

**Via Yeovil**

This is Devonport King's Road looking toward Bere Alston on the same day. It was closed on 7 September 1964 when the line as far as St Budeaux was completely closed as part of a scheme to eliminate duplication of services and reduce costs. Today the site of the station is occupied by Plymouth College of Further Education. Alignment of the 'past' and 'present' views was aided by the existence of the old approach road (on the extreme right) and a road overbridge in the background. *H. C. Casserley/TG*

19

The line entered a tunnel under Devonport Park just beyond Devonport station, at the other end of which was Albert Road Halt. This was opened in 1906 as part of a scheme to provide a commuter service within the Plymouth area; it closed in 1947. The line then entered another tunnel before reaching Ford. This view of Ford, looking south, was taken in BR days.

The exact location of the station is difficult to identify today, but clues include the remains of the up-side entrance (right of the photograph), the adjacent houses and those in the background. The other landmark seen in both photographs is the building with the asymmetric roof behind the concrete platelayers' hut. The cutting has been filled in and a public park and new houses have been built. *Lens of Sutton/TG*

Another halt was provided at Camel's Head, which opened in 1906 and closed in 1942. The remains of the halt were left for many years, but today there is no longer any trace of it, although its location is easily deduced from the surrounding houses. The present-day photograph of the site of Camel's Head Halt was taken from a lower elevation because the bridge carrying the railway over a road has been demolished and the embankment removed.

Yet another halt, just over a quarter of a mile further on at Weston Mill, was also built in 1906. It closed in 1921 and no trace remains. Just past Weston Mill the line ran for a short distance parallel with the GWR line through St Budeaux (see page 24). *Lens of Sutton/TG*

# The present (former GWR) route to St Budeaux

There was a halt at Wingfield Villas, but the first station proper on the GWR line from Plymouth North Road was Devonport Albert Road, very close to the LSWR's Albert Road Halt. The station has changed little over the years as this comparison shows. The main station building has gone, but the station is still open, served by trains to Gunnislake and slow trains to Liskeard and further west. On 7 May 1999 the 10.35 from Gunnislake to Plymouth is operated by Class 150 No 150267. The next station is Devonport Dockyard, also still open and served by the same trains. *Courtesy Lens of Sutton/TG*

*Right* The station has been enhanced by local artists, as this plaque commemorates. *TG*

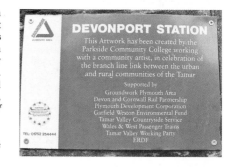

DEVONPORT STATION

This Artwork has been created by the Parkside Community College working with a community artist, in celebration of the branch line link between the urban and rural communities of the Tamar

Supported by
Groundwork Plymouth Area
Devon and Cornwall Rail Partnership
Plymouth Development Corporation
Garfield Weston Environmental Fund
Tamar Valley Countryside Service
Wales & West Passenger Trains
Tamar Valley Working Party
ERDF

TEL: 01752 254444

A short distance further on was Ford Platform, seen here in GWR days before closure on 6 October 1941. There are still some remains of the platforms, and the 1999 view looking in the same direction shows two Class 37s on a ballast train. In the background is Devonport Dockyard station. The Royal Naval Dockyards themselves are to the right-hand (west) side of the railway line.

The next station is Keyham, which is still open, and is only a quarter of a mile behind the camera. The line then passes over Weston Mill Viaduct to meet the LSWR line just before the two St Budeaux stations, which are adjacent. There was no physical connection between the two lines until 1941, when a spur was built to aid the flow of wartime traffic. Since closure of the LSWR route from Plymouth in 1964, trains for Bere Alston and Gunnislake have used this spur to gain access to the former LSWR main line. The GWR line turns west and passes into Cornwall over the Royal Albert Bridge at Saltash. *Courtesy Lens of Sutton/TG*

# St Budeaux to Bere Alston

This is looking south from the down platform at St Budeaux Victoria Road; the GWR station of Ferry Road is in a cutting beyond the building on the right-hand side.

Present-day Victoria Road station is rather bare, with only the old up platform surviving. The junction with the former LSWR route under the bridge has been removed. The line was singled to Bere Alston in 1970, and on 8 May 1999 Class 150 No 150244 pauses on the 08.15 from Gunnislake. The line falls at 1 in 75 to a point just beyond the next station, Tamerton Foliot. *Lens of Sutton/TG*

The ex-LSWR line passes under the ex-GWR main line just past St Budeaux station, then again at the Royal Albert Bridge, and finally under the modern Tamar Bridge carrying the A38. The outskirts of Plymouth are left behind as the line runs along the edge of the River Tamar, past sidings laid in 1938 to serve the adjacent Admiralty Depot, to Tamerton Bridge, where on 12 August 1991 Class 108 No 955 works the 11.30 Plymouth to Gunnislake service. *TG*

Just after crossing the bridge was Tamerton Foliot station. The village is over a mile east along Station Road, which skirts the northern edge of Tamerton Lake. The station was opened as Tamerton Foliott in December 1897, and the spelling was changed to Foliot in 1906. The station was demoted to a halt in 1959, as seen in the 'past' photograph, and closed on 10 September 1962.

The station building is now a private house, and the remains of the platforms are still clearly visible in this April 1999 photograph. Station Road is a cul-de-sac that ends at the station. Beyond here a track over the bridge leads to Warleigh Wood and a nature reserve. *Lens of Sutton/TG*

Good views of Tamerton Foliot Lake can be had at various points along Station Road. This 1914 view of the eastern end of the lake shows boathouses on the left and the village in the background.

The view has changed little over the decades. Note the decaying remains of a boat on the left. By contrast the village itself has changed a lot, with much expansion on to the surrounding hillside. Even the centre has changed, with demolition of some of the older houses. *Author's collection/TG*

The Tavy Bridge was longer than that at Tamerton, as can be seen in this photograph taken on 4 August 1960. 'West Country' Class No 34104, appropriately named *Bere Alston*, has just crossed the River Tavy on the last stages of its journey from Waterloo, which it left at 9.00am, and is due to arrive at Plymouth at 3.15pm. This train had split at Exeter Central, with the rear portion going forward to Ilfracombe.

The former down line was later removed, and on 12 August 1991 DMU Class 108 No 955 forms the 12.40 Gunnislake to Plymouth. *Hugh Ballantyne/TG*

Bere Ferrers station is situated on the edge of the village and has as a result always been better used than Tamerton Foliot. Being on the peninsula between the Tamar and Tavy, road access is much more difficult and this a further incentive to use the trains. The distance to Plymouth City Centre by rail is 8 miles and by road 23 miles, the first part being very narrow and the latter congested major roads. By walking a mile west from the station, the River Tamar is reached at Thorn Point, while half a mile east brings the walker to the River Tavy at Bere Ferrers Quay. On 14 August 1969, before rationalisation of the main line, a DMU stops at Bere Ferrers on the 1.15pm Plymouth to Gunnislake.

A visit on the evening of 5 May 1999 found that some unusual changes had taken place. The goods yard was occupied by some ex-LNER coaches and other rolling-stock, and on the platform was an ex-LSWR signal box, which had not been there on previous visits. The station building and yard are privately owned, as is the signal box, which had been brought from Pinhoe, the original having been at the other end of the station. There is also a collection of smaller railway 'ironmongery'. The owner offers evening meals during the summer months and these are served in a railway carriage known as the 'Tamar Belle' – advance booking is required. A visitor centre is housed in a former LMS sleeping carriage in the station yard. The 17.15 from Gunnislake to Plymouth is operated by Class 150 No 150267. These units and those of Class 153 were introduced on this line in 1992. *Ronald Lumber/TG*

*Opposite* A better view of Bere Ferrers goods yard is obtained from the south end of the station. The yard was closed in 1965 and the track subsequently removed, as seen on 22 August 1989. Another visit on 26 May 1992 found the track re-instated under its new ownership. DMU Class 108 No 955 (again) forms the 11.50 from Plymouth to Gunnislake. In the mornings trains to Plymouth made mandatory stops here, but afternoon trains stopped only on request. The converse applied to trains to Gunnislake. Now (2001) all trains stop here only on request. *Both TG*

The line climbs through Bere Ferrers at 1 in 73, and beyond the station leaves the low-lying area of the peninsula to enter an attractive wooded area before continuing to climb almost all the way to Bere Alston. On 22 August 1989 Set No 871 approaches Bere Ferrers on the 12.40 Gunnislake to Plymouth. This is an odd set made up of one coach of Class 101 and one of Class 108. These and similar vehicles were transferred from the North of England following withdrawal in 1986 of the new railbuses of Class 142, which were found to be unsuitable. *TG*

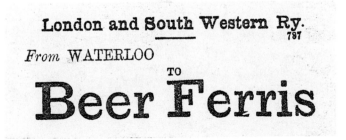

An LSWR luggage label – note the spelling.

Bere Ferrers.

Bere Ferrers is a very attractive village, well worth a visit. This is the approach to the quay depicted on an old postcard, the approximate date of which can be deduced from the absence of the war memorial seen in the present-day photograph and the request to affix a halfpenny postage stamp to the card.

Little else has changed in the village, although the coming of the telephone has resulted in the usual clutter of poles and cables. An extension on the end of the nearest house is the Post Office, while on the other side of the road one of the houses is now the Plough Inn. Day-trippers from Plymouth used to travel by paddle-steamer to Bere Ferrers, but present-day trippers can use the train. *Author's Collection/TG*

After about 2 miles the railway, which is still running northward, passes under Furzehill Bridge. At this location in September 1957 is Class O2 No 30193 on a Plymouth to Tavistock North train consisting of two ex-LSWR coaches.

Despite the passage of time, this location is easily identified. Unfortunately the exact position from where the past photograph was taken is not accessible to the public, but a public footpath runs from the road overbridge down the side of the cutting and crosses the railway at a point just behind the rear coach of the steam train. It was from here that the present-day photograph was taken, showing Class 150 No 150267 forming the 16.25 from Plymouth to Gunnislake on 5 May 1999. *Colin Hogg, courtesy Mike Esau/TG*

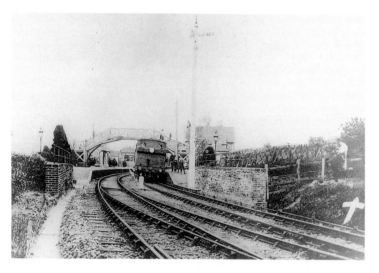

The line curves sharply to the east on the approach to Bere Alston, and the station itself, which lies at right-angles to Bere Ferrers, is on the curve. These three photographs span about 80 years. In the first an O2 Class engine waits in the down main platform on a train from Tavistock. The centre photograph, taken on 20 July 1970, shows that the footbridge and wooden post signal have both been replaced with iron versions, although no significant changes have been made to the station buildings. By May 1992 the up main line, the semaphore signal and the footbridge have all been removed, while just beyond the station the old down main line terminates at a buffer stop. The train, consisting of Set No 955, is the 12.40 from Gunnislake, which reverses here before proceeding to Plymouth. *Courtesy Lens of Sutton/ D. J. Aston/TG*

Looking in the other direction the branch to Gunnislake and Callington can be seen, and in this photograph, taken in the late 1950s, Class O2 No 30225 is approaching Bere Alston station; the main line is immediately to the left out of view.

The track layout at Bere Alston was altered in 1970, when the branch bay was closed and a direct connection made to the old main line. In this view, of Set No 955 approaching Bere Alston on 25 May 1992, the connection is immediately behind the camera, with the main line in the foreground. DMUs replaced steam engines from 7 September 1964. *Mike Esau/TG*

Further views from the west end of the station, the first showing the main line. In the summer of 1958 a train to Exeter enters the station in the hands of Class T9 No 30711 of Exmouth Junction Shed. The first two coaches constitute Bulleid Set No 70, behind which is a Maunsell coach, then another Bulleid coach, all main-line corridor stock. In the background is the branch line and beyond this the goods yard.

The same location on 14 August 1969 shows the 11.25am DMU from Plymouth leaving on the branch after reversing.

The present simplified layout is seen in the third photograph with Class 150 No 150267 approaching from the branch on 5 May 1999. The railway cottages in the background of the two previous views are still there, but have become obscured by trees. *Mike Esau/Ronald Lumber/TG*

London and South Western Ry.

787

*From* WATERLOO

TO

# BEER ALSTON

The Callington train, as usual headed by a Class O2 locomotive, waits in the branch bay at Bere Alston in the late 1950s. Much of the platform and trackbed is now overgrown, as seen in the spring of 1999. A Sunday service was operated between 1924 and 1962, re-instated during the summer seasons from 1983 to 1987, and again from 1990 to the present time. *Mike Esau/TG*

The village centre is just over half a mile south-east of the station along a road, as usual called Station Road. This is the village end of Station Road, looking toward the station in 1905. It is amazing how little this scene has changed – a study of the 1999 photograph shows the wheelwright's yard and buildings still in existence on the right, while on the other side a footpath has been added. A solitary sodium lamp lights the corner and surprisingly there are no telegraph poles. *Author's Collection/TG*

# Bere Alston to Gunnislake

On leaving Bere Alston the line takes several sharp curves and descends steeply at 1 in 39 to reach the viaduct over the River Tamar at Calstock. A comprehensive photographic record of the building of Calstock Viaduct exists and this photograph shows the viaduct and the approach from the Devon side under construction in August 1907.

Much of the line is now hemmed in by trees and hedges, but there is a gap that enables the viaduct to be seen from the same position. On 8 October 1999 Class 150 No 150230 has just crossed the viaduct on the 14.35 from Gunnislake to Plymouth. Calstock station is in Cornwall at the far end of the viaduct. *Calstock Parish Archive/TG*

Before the coming of the railway there were regular sailings to and from Plymouth along the Tamar, and two paddle-steamers are moored against Calstock Quay in this turn-of-the-century photograph. The building of the viaduct resulted in the piers intruding into this view, and in 1999 it can be seen that several buildings have been added, in particular a Methodist chapel visible between the first and second piers from the right. *Calstock Parish Archive/TG*

A position high above the river on the Cornwall side gives an excellent view of progress on construction of the viaduct in the early summer of 1907. The blocks are concrete and were cast on site. Beyond the piers on the Devon side is a boatyard, where many of the craft on the Tamar were constructed. The elegance of the completed viaduct is caught in the second photograph taken on 4 July 1961 of Class 2MT No 41317 on the 4.23pm from Callington to Plymouth. *Calstock Parish Archive/TG*

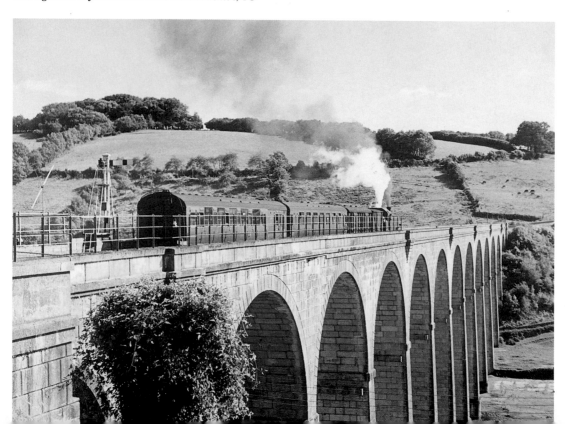

Equally impressive views of the viaduct can be had further away at river level. The 'past' photograph shows the viaduct nearing completion, and a wagon lift to connect the quayside sidings to the new line over the viaduct is under construction. Some way behind the camera, the East Cornwall Mineral Railway turned inland up a 1 in 6 incline to The Butts (see page 55). Horses were used to haul wagons along the quayside to the incline, where they were hauled by rope operated by a stationary engine; some of the incline is still accessible.

Boats still moor along here and there is plenty of evidence of the mineral line, long since closed. A footpath that follows the river leads to Cotehele. The remains of the lift, which was dismantled in about 1934, can also been seen on closer inspection of the viaduct. *Calstock Parish Archive/TG*

This photograph of the boatbuilding yard on the Devon bank was taken in April 1906 during construction of the viaduct. The boatyard closed after the viaduct was built and the site is now occupied by Ferry Farm. The ferry also ceased regular workings when the railway opened, but was later re-instated and ran until 1967. It began running again on an experimental basis during the summer of 1998. A ferry service between Calstock and Cotehele, calling at Ferry Farm on request, began operating from the summer of 1999, providing a very pleasant way to reach the National Trust house of the same name. A new landing stage was installed at Calstock in 2000.
*Calstock Parish Archive/TG*

This turn-of-the-century photograph was taken from Ashburton Hill, just to the west of Calstock village, looking down river toward Plymouth. Cotehele Quay, where there is a museum of river traffic, is just beyond the bend. Little change has taken place here as shown by the 1999 view from the same place. *Calstock Parish Archive/TG*

The 'past' view shows Calstock station not long after opening, with the viaduct and wagon lift beyond. This vista is blocked in summer by foliage, but a visit in the spring of 1999 gave a clearer view. The wagon lift and sidings have gone and a house erected at the end of the goods yard. No platform was ever provided in the loop, which has now been taken out. Access to the station from this side had been closed for many years, but was re-instated at the end of 2000. The station building was to the same design as those on the Kent & East Sussex Railway (see the *Past and Present Companion* listed in the Bibliography). *Courtesy Lens of Sutton/TG*

Calstock station is on a sharp curve, as seen here on 3 July 1961 with the 4.23pm Callington to Bere Alston train hauled by Class 2MT No 41317. These engines of LMS design first appeared in the area in 1952 to replace the ex-PDSWJR engines. Class O2 engines continued to be used on most passenger trains until they were also displaced by the 2MTs about 1961, which were in turn replaced by diesels in 1964. One such DMU, No B461 of Class 118, is seen at the station on 19 August 1986. *Both TG*

Calstock village is built on a hill and the various narrow roads within the village drop steeply toward the river. This is Wesleyan Road in 1930, which obviously led to the chapel. The same road today is called Back Lane and the chapel has been converted into living accommodation called Wesley Flats. *Author's Collection/TG*

On leaving Calstock the train continues to climb and snake round the sharp curves to the squeal of wheel flanges. The line is hemmed in on both sides and at this point it is difficult to believe that a standard gauge train can pass. In the foreground is an ungated crossing carrying a minor road, typical of those in the area. Immediately to the right, out of view, is the road that leads to Harewood Farm and Okel Tor. On 22 August 1989 Class 101/108 No 871 appears from nowhere on the 14.35 from Gunnislake to Plymouth. *TG*

Okel Tor Mine was about half a mile east of Calstock and opened in 1848. It closed in 1874, re-opened in 1881, but was abandoned in 1887, several years before the railway to Callington opened. The mine was close to the River Tamar (and even under the river), and ore was taken out by barge. Not surprisingly there are very few photographs of the mine, and they are of poor quality. This undated photograph gives an indication of the size of the operation.

The old buildings still stand today; some have been restored and others are in a dilapidated state. The hillside is covered in trees and gorse and exploring is a little hazardous. The remains can be viewed, at least in winter, from one of the several nearby public footpaths, although the buildings themselves are on private land. The 'past' and 'present' views were aligned using the footpath and chimney (top left) as markers. *Calstock Parish Archive/TG*

This location, showing the railway under construction, was difficult to find, but was eventually traced to a point immediately after a bridge that carries a track to Harewood Farm. The clues were the cutting in the foreground and the contour of the hill in the background. The same spot was visited on 4 April 1999 when a train bound for Gunnislake (not Plymouth as on the indicator panel) squeezed its way round the curve. In summer this view is completely blocked by foliage. *Courtesy Lens of Sutton/TG*

A few hundred yards further east it is possible in winter to see the River Tamar in the valley below, and Morwellham Quay on the Devon bank. The 'past' view, taken in about 1870, shows the extent of the Quay, while in the background are the buildings associated with the works and cottages for the workers. The road in the background is the only way into Morwellham by land and leads to the main Gunnislake to Tavistock road. Also in the background are the tramways from the Tavistock Canal and the Devon Great Consols Mine, which around the Quay are elevated.

The tramway closed in 1899 and the Quay was virtually abandoned by 1903, when the tramway was sold for scrap. However, in 1969 restoration began and the second photograph, taken in January 2001, shows the reconstructed Quay with the elevated tramway and the restored ketch *Garlandstone*, built in 1909 at Calstock (see page 44). *Courtesy of the Morwellham and Tamar Valley Trust/TG*

On leaving Hare Wood the railway passes St Andrew's Church and runs adjacent to the road from Calstock to Drakewalls. The 3.15pm from Bere Alston to Callington runs along this section of the line on 28 June 1956 behind a Class O2. On 22 August 1989 Class 101/108 No 871 forms the 13.45 from Plymouth to Gunnislake and is seen from the other side of the road at the same location. *J. H. Aston/TG*

In September 1957 a Callington-bound train approaches an ungated crossing 1 mile south of Gunnislake; the engine is Class O2 No 30216. The platelayers' hut still stands and the crossing is still ungated, but trains are required to stop before proceeding. This present-day view, showing Class 150 No 150248 on the 16.25 from Plymouth on 6 May 1999, is seen through a telephoto lens, which accentuates the curves. *Colin Hogg, courtesy Mike Esau/TG*

The ECMR had two 0-4-0 saddle tanks, which were used between the top of the incline at The Butts and Kelly Bray. Following the opening of the line from Bere Alston to Callington, these engines were converted to standard gauge 0-4-2s, and engine No 2, seen here at The Butts, was sold to the Hundred of Manhood & Selsey Tramway in 1912. To the right is the engine shed and further right (in the present-day photograph) the water tower. After lying abandoned for decades, the buildings have been restored and are in use by a removal company, which the author has himself used. *Courtesy Doris Sleeman/TG*

Trainer Bridge is beyond The Butts yard of the ECMR and this illustration shows the construction of the railway in 1872, with a new overbridge carrying the road from Calstock to Drakewalls. The intersection of the two lines was a few yards to the north, but there was no junction, as the ECMR line from here to Calstock was closed following the building of the new line from Bere Alston. The ECMR cutting has been partly filled in at this point, as seen in January 2001. *Courtesy Doris Sleeman/TG*

The present day-view from road level is more interesting and shows the course of the incline through the gates. In the left background is an abandoned chimney of Wheal Edward, the associated buildings of which are in use as a private residence. *TG*

About half a mile beyond Trainer Bridge is the village of Albaston. This 1930s photograph shows some rather austere buildings, which are still in use and their appearance has been greatly improved. The 1960s car belies the fact that the second photograph was taken in 1999. *Calstock Village Archive/TG*

*Opposite* Looking south from Gunnislake station on 4 July 1961 witnesses the departure for Bere Alston of the 6.15pm from Callington. The engine is Class 2MT No 41317. In the background by the tall tree is the bridge carrying the railway over the main Callington to Tavistock road (A390).

The same location in the summer of 2000 shows that the area is very much overgrown and the track lifted. In the background the row of cottages still exist. *Both TG*

By walking through the undergrowth toward the bridge, dramatic changes are revealed. The bridge has been removed and there is a new bus/train interchange point, opened on 8 June 1994, but the cottages provide a link with the previous photographs. The reason for resiting the station was primarily because of the low height of the bridge. The track was realigned slightly to the right and at a lower level. The train is the 13.50 from Plymouth on 12 January 2001. *TG*

SOUTHERN RAILWAY.

(8/25)

Stock
787

TO

GUNNISLAKE

Looking toward Callington on 23 July 1964, this train, which started at Gunnislake, left for Bere Alston at 2.24pm, on this occasion hauled by Class 2MT No 41308 shortly before diesels took over.

Following closure beyond Gunnislake on 7 November 1966, the track was removed from the goods yard and one face of the island platform, and a substitute bus service ran until 1972. There is currently a bi-hourly bus service from Tavistock to Callington via the new station, Calstock Quay and Harrowbarrow. On 19 August 1986 Class 118 No 461 forms the 12.09 to Plymouth.

The third view shows all that remained in 1999, including the sodium lamps that replaced the much more attractive gas lamps installed by the SR and the oil lamps before them. *J. H. Aston/TG (2)*

This is the 6.01pm from Bere Alston at Gunnislake on 4 July 1961, where it terminated. Although advertised as starting from Bere Alston, in fact this train ran from Plymouth, leaving at 5.10pm, arriving at Bere Alston at 5.43pm. The only other train to terminate at Gunnislake was the 1.58pm from Bere Alston, which only ran on Wednesdays, Thursdays and Saturdays. The station was built on the former Drakewalls Depot of the ECMR. The last passenger train to use the station ran on 29 January 1994 and all that remains today is the station approach road and the platform. *Both TG*

The line entered a short cutting just beyond Gunnislake station and continued to climb until just before Luckett. This is the 5.23pm from Bere Alston on 4 July 1961 with Class 2MT No 41317 on the front of the train. The cutting is still accessible, at least in winter, and the bridge carrying a minor road over the railway is still in use. *Both TG*

Gunnislake stations (old and new) are both in the village of Drakewalls, and not Gunnislake. The main road starts to descend steeply at the western end of Drakewalls, as seen in this old photograph. The railway is situated at the other end of the village, the old station being on the left and the new station on the right.

The present-day photograph of the same row of houses shows that the one in the foreground has become a hairdressing salon. The road sign in the background warns of the steepening gradient, and beyond this sign another advises of a sharp left-hand curve. *Calstock Village Archive/TG*

By continuing down the hill past the stations for a further three-quarters of a mile, Gunnislake village is reached. This 1950s photograph of the centre of the village shows the main road, at this point called Fore Street, surprisingly quiet.

Little has changed over the decades, apart from a huge increase in through traffic and the installation of traffic lights to control vehicles passing along the narrowest part of Fore Street. The Commercial Hotel has become the Cornish Inn, while the shop advertising Lyons Tea on the extreme left is now a fish and chip shop, and the first building on the right has become a bank. *Author's Collection/TG*

Dimson, immediately to the west of Gunnislake, consists of four communities known as Higher, Middle, North and Lower Dimson, all owing their existence predominantly to the proximity of mines and quarries. This view, looking north from the hillside, shows Lower Dimson. In the top left-hand corner the 'coliseum' is in fact the kiln of the Plymouth Brick Works, long since demolished.

The row of houses in the foreground was surprisingly difficult to find, as the 'past' photograph had no identifying text to determine even the direction of the view. The closer present-day view was necessitated because the hillside is now completely covered by mature trees. Buildings now occupy most of the open land in the middle ground, the bottom part being a recreation ground. The building in the centre with the bell is Gunnislake Primary School. *Calstock Village Archive/TG*

# Gunnislake to Callington

Chilsworthy, opened on 1 June 1909, was only 1 mile beyond Gunnislake and a short walk from North Dimson. A Callington-bound train hauled by one of the three locomotives built for the PDSWJR is seen here shortly after opening of the line. Note the interesting signal where a single post is used for displaying arms for both directions; these are to indicate to the driver whether there are any intending passengers. The same system was used on the Kent & East Sussex Railway, as Colonel Stephens was the engineer of both railways. There was some ambivalence as to the status of Chilsworthy on the part of both the Southern Railway and British Railways, as it was shown as a station in the public timetable but as a halt on some tickets.

The station retained its oil lamps right up to the line's closure on 7 November 1966, and the second photograph shows the deserted platform on 4 July 1961.

Today the trackbed is used as a public footpath. The remains of the platform can be found in the undergrowth. There were also sidings for coal and a brickworks, but there is no trace of these.

*Courtesy Lens of Sutton/TG (2)*

Between Chilsworthy and Latchley were sidings serving Hingston Down quarries, which are still open. This is Latchley looking toward Chilsworthy in the 1950s. By this time the siding to a loading dock on the left had been removed; this is the site of the ECMR's Cox's Park Depot. Today the station is on private land and the owners have retained the platform. *Courtesy Lens of Sutton/TG*

Looking in the other direction can be seen milepost 6½ on the platform and the ungated crossing beyond. Today's view shows a pleasant, well-maintained area, with the edge of the old station house just visible on the right.
*Courtesy Lens of Sutton/TG*

A halt known as Seven Stones was located between Latchley and Luckett; opened in 1910, it closed after only seven years. It was not built to bring workmen to the mines and brickworks in the area, but to bring day-trippers to an adjacent pleasure park. Just over a mile to the south at Harrowbarrow was the Prince of Wales Mine. This had opened in the 16th century for the extraction of silver and later also yielded copper, tin and arsenic. It closed in 1916 and this old photograph shows the surface workings. The remains of these buildings can still be seen and there are even some short lengths of narrow gauge track. As with all mining areas, caution needs to be exercised because of the disused shafts. *Calstock Village Archive/TG*

The 1.00pm from Callington to Bere Alston enters Luckett on 4 July 1961 behind Class 2MT No 41317. The loop on the right has no platform and was used by goods trains. The road over the railway leads to Luckett village. On the extreme right is the station house. The trackbed and platforms can still be clearly seen, as in this photograph taken in April 1999. *Both TG*

Stoke Climsland Station

Luckett, on the site of the ECMR's Monk's Corner Depot, served the village of the same name, which is just over a mile to the north. The station was, however, opened as Stoke Climsland, to be renamed 18 months later; the nearest station to Stoke Climsland was Callington, a distance of 2 miles.

The second photograph shows that Luckett is unchanged after half a century, apart from the loss of one siding. Even the wooden fencing has survived.

The view is still immediately recognisable in 2000. The track has of course gone, but the station survives as holiday accommodation. *Courtesy Lens of Sutton/J. H. Aston/TG*

## London and South Western Ry.

787

### FROM WATERLOO TO

# LUCKETT

The village of Luckett is approached down a steep hill from which there are views of the surrounding mine workings. In 1904 Wheal Martha was photographed from a field on the hillside just to the west of this road. The cottage marked with a cross just right of centre is where the Methodist denomination was founded in East Cornwall. The cottage was demolished in 1914 and a house with a Post Office built on the site. Records mention workings in the nearby mines in 1764, Wheal Martha itself being abandoned in 1878. It re-opened for the extraction of tin in 1949, but closed permanently three years later.

The view from the same location in 1999 shows that nature has reclaimed the land on which the mine was situated and only a few of the buildings remain. *Courtesy Yvonne King/TG*

Callington, Church Hill.

Beyond Luckett there was a siding serving a quarry tramway as the line skirted the northern edge of Kit Hill before reaching the terminus at Kelly Bray, formerly used by the ECMR. This was named Callington Road by the PDSWJR, the town being over a mile to the south. This is an almost deserted Church Hill in the town of Callington in about 1904.

Most of these buildings are still in existence and the cobbled frontages have been retained. A careful study shows that the first house on the right has lost its front porch, and an ugly flat-roofed extension ruins the building in front of St Mary's Church. Horse-buses used to run between Tavistock and Liskeard under the auspices of the LSWR, and the GWR ran horse-buses and later motor-buses from Callington to Saltash, but both services were withdrawn once the railway opened. In 1961 the reverse occurred when buses were introduced between Callington and Plymouth via the new Saltash road bridge over the River Tamar to Plymouth. Church Hill is now called Church Street, but the road to the right has retained its unusual name of Zaggy Lane. *Author's Collection/TG*

Callington Station.

London and South Western Ry.

787

WATERLOO TO

# CALLINGTON ROAD

This early view from the end of the platform at Callington Road station shows a train from Bere Alston approaching, with the engine shed to the immediate left. The station was renamed Callington for Stoke Climsland in 1909, and plain Callington from the 1950s. In 1928 the platform was lengthened and the entrance to the engine shed was relocated at the other

end of the building. In the background is Kit Hill, with the chimney of the summit mine; the chimney is still a major landmark and the hill is a popular place to explore.

The changes to the engine shed are shown in the second photograph, which was taken in about 1960, but by 1970 the engine shed had been demolished and the track removed. The site was subsequently redeveloped for industrial use and is now called Beeching Park, as the notice at the entrance on the left in the 'present' view shows. *Courtesy Lens of Sutton (2)/J. H. Aston/TG*

The attractive overall roof of the station frames the 1.00pm train to Bere Alston on 4 July 1961. The main road from Launceston to Callington itself passes from right to left beyond the buffer stops in the background.

A scene of desolation greeted the photographer on 17 August 1970, and 30 years later the site is still far from attractive. The road in the foreground, which crosses the site of the platform end, leads to the industrial estate. Outside the former railway property, the houses to the right, the long shed beyond, and the houses on the main road still stand. *TG/J. H. Aston/ TG*

# Bere Alston to Meldon Junction (Okehampton)

Beyond Bere Alston the main line rose at 1 in 75 and ran north-east until it reached the River Tavy. In September 1957 a GWR engine, Class 4300 No 6394, takes a train of SR coaches and vans to Plymouth.

The route was closed on 6 May 1968, and this section of the line is now very overgrown, making identification of the 'past' locations difficult. A visit in the spring of 1999 found the trackbed impassable in many places, but this photograph is of the same location as far as can be judged by the proximity of the road overbridge. *Colin Hogg, courtesy Mike Esau/TG*

Having reached the Tavy, the line turns north and follows the river into Tavistock, but at a much higher elevation. At first it falls at 1 in 98, followed by a climb at 1 in 75 through Tavistock. Just before Tavistock the line is carried over the main Callington to Tavistock road, and it was from this point that the 7.15am Plymouth Friary to Exeter Central was seen on 9 July 1958. The engine is, appropriately, 'West Country' Class No 34104 *Bere Alston*. The road overbridge had been demolished and the allotment is overgrown, as seen in March 2001. *Both TG*

**The approach to Tavistock is through a cutting, and seen here on 8 July 1958 is Class T9 No 30710 on the 7.00am from Okehampton to Plymouth Friary. Today the trackbed is used as a public footpath, so locating this point in 1999 was not difficult.** *Both TG*

Immediately before Tavistock station is a magnificent viaduct carrying the line high above the town, which lies to the south. In the valley on the other side of town was the GWR line from Plymouth to Launceston, much of which ran parallel to the LSWR line from Tavistock to Lydford. On 4 August 1960 the Plymouth portion of the 'Atlantic Coast Express' crosses the viaduct behind Class N No 31846, although express passenger trains were usually hauled by 'West Country' 'Pacifics'. The footpath seen in the previous photograph continues over the viaduct, as seen in the 1999 photograph. *Hugh Ballantyne/TG*

This is Tavistock station seen from the viaduct end, probably in the 1930s. The oil lamps were subsequently replaced by electric lights using the old cast-iron posts, and some were later replaced by the SR with concrete posts.

Since closure much of the station area has been redeveloped and houses have been built across the trackbed at the end of the viaduct, making it difficult to re-open the line into the old station. It was originally proposed to build the station at the west end of the viaduct, and it would be ironic if this was where a new station was built, in the event of the line being re-opened. The stone walls on either side of the footpath are the end of the viaduct.
*Courtesy Lens of Sutton/TG*

The other end of the station on 5 June 1959 finds a freight train bound for Exeter in the hands of Class N No 31845. Ten years later demolition was under way – the up side was cleared, but the canopy survives on the Launceston Steam Railway and the footbridge on the Plym Valley Railway, while the down platform, its canopy and the main station building were retained. All this, together with the small yard, passed into private ownership to become the home of the former station master and his wife, and they named it 'Beeching's Folly'. The station master's widow continued to live here until her death in 1998; she had a beautiful Humber classic car that she would display on the station forecourt during the author's visits. The station continues to be a private residence. *J. H. Aston/D. J. Aston/TG*

Looking toward Okehampton from the platform end on 5 June 1959 finds a down freight train involved in shunting movements on the up line, adjacent to which was the main goods yard. The land is now occupied by the offices and car park of West Devon Borough Council, and this photograph, taken from the same position in the summer of 1999, shows little evidence of the railway. *J. H. Aston/TG*

Judging by the Royal Mail delivery van outside the Post Office, this view of the centre of Tavistock from the Abbey Bridge over the River Tavy is probably from the 1920s. It is certainly post-1918, as there is a war memorial in Guildhall Square, to the right. Next to this is Bedford Square, where there is a statue of Francis, Duke of Bedford, erected in 1864. The pannier market, which is well worth a visit, is behind these buildings, and the tower is that of the parish church of St Eustachius. The road in the middle distance between the shops leads under the viaduct to the former LSWR station, while the GWR line passes behind the photographer on the east bank of the river. The 'present' view is equally attractive and all the buildings remain in good order. *Author's Collection/TG*

There used to be an iron foundry in Tavistock, which opened in 1805 and has long since closed. Little remains on the site, which at the time of the author's visit was scheduled for redevelopment into houses and offices; however, a modern replica of a traditional gas lamp acts as a reminder of the past. The foundry was responsible for the ironwork at Tavistock station, and amazingly one station lamp-post to an LSWR pattern and cast at the foundry has survived, its origins clearly visible after 110 years. *Both TG*

A little beyond Tavistock the line dropped at 1 in 90 and passed over the GWR line, which had crossed to the west bank of the River Tavy. The two lines then ran side by side along the east bank of the River Burn. A Southern Region train from Plymouth is seen on this section in the late 1950s, consisting of 'West Country' Class No 34106 *Lydford* and BR Mark I coaches of Set No 888. The GWR line is in the right background.

Although both lines have now gone, there is still plenty of evidence of the former railways, including an SR concrete platelayers' hut. This is close to Mary Tavy, where only the GWR had a station. *Mike Esau/TG*

The first station out of Tavistock on the LSWR line was Brentor, which was visited in July 1967, almost a year before closure. The GWR had no station here and its line ran immediately to the right just out of the photograph. Brentor station has been beautifully restored, as seen in the summer 1999 photograph, and is in use as a private residence. *Both TG*

In BR days there was one train a day that ran only from Plymouth to Brentor, with a balancing return working. The latter, the 5.30pm to Plymouth Friary on 28 June 1956, is formed of Class M7 No 30037, Bulleid two-coach corridor Set No 68, and a loose coach on the rear.

Today the trackbed has been filled in, although the platform faces are still clearly identifiable at the present time. The road overbridges were removed in 1989 and the cuttings filled in, another barrier to the possible re-opening of the line. *J. H. Aston/TG*

At Lydford the two railway companies had adjacent stations, close to Lydford Gorge. This view, looking south on 29 July 1969, shows the LSWR line, with the GWR to the right. By this time both stations had closed, the GWR's at the end of 1962 and the LSWR's in May 1968. Separate approach roads led to the two stations from either side of the nearby road overbridges carrying the Lydford to Brentor road. There were also extensive sidings installed during the Second World War, but little trace of these remains.

Today the site has changed out of all recognition and much is inaccessible because it is overgrown and also privately owned. The 'present' view was aligned with the 'past' by the building seen on the extreme right. *D. J. Aston/TG*

## London and South Western Ry.

787

From_____

TO

# LIDFORD

An LSWR luggage label – note the spelling.

Looking north from the end of the GWR station at Lydford in April 1960 sees Class 4500 No 5569 approaching with a train from Launceston to Plymouth. The two railways parted company here, the GWR line turning sharply to the west beyond the signal, and the LSWR continuing north toward Okehampton on the right.

The main identifying features on a visit on 20 August 1987 were the GWR platform and the house on higher ground in the background. This view has since been obliterated by further growth of trees. *Mike Esau/TG*

From Lydford the line rose at 1 in 78 to Bridestowe. The village is 1¾ miles to the west, nestling among the hills, as shown in this old photograph.

The present-day view is most unusually less impeded by natural growth. Bridestowe is a most pleasant and attractive village, benefiting from the construction of a bypass in recent years. The new road runs east to west and is indicated by the sodium lamps at the edge of the field beyond the village. *Author's Collection/TG*

Bridestowe station is seen from the road overbridge on 4 May 1968, as an afternoon Exeter to Plymouth train calls. Today most of the buildings have been retained and are in a first-class state of repair under private ownership. The main Tavistock to Okehampton road crosses the railway on a bridge half a mile north of the station. A tramway, built in 1879 to carry peat from the moor, but dismantled in 1931/32, had a siding adjacent to the main line at this point. *Ronald Lumber/TG*

A reminder that this was once a main line is the passage of the Plymouth to Brighton train through Bridestowe in the summer of 1964, hauled by 'West Country' Class No 34106 *Lydford*. It left Plymouth at 11.10am, calling at Devonport and Tavistock North, then Okehampton, Exeter and major stations to Salisbury and Southampton, arriving at Brighton at 5.24pm. The last Plymouth to Brighton train ran on 4 March 1967. All is now quiet at this and most other stations between Plymouth and Exeter.

Shortly after Bridestowe the highest point on the SR was reached at Sourton. The line then descended past Meldon Junction to Okehampton. *Lawrence Golden/TG*

# INDEX OF LOCATIONS